This book is especially for
Rye, Bud, Karen, Gay and Alden Vervaet
who held in their mind the memory of the land
as it was and have returned it to us
to be loved by all.
Special thanks to Mag-la-Que,
Mahte-Topah, and Miyaca

No part of this publication may be reproduced in whole or in part, or
stored in a retrieval system, or transmitted in any form or by any
means, electronic, mechanical, photocopying, recording, or
otherwise, without written permission of the publisher. For
information regarding permission, write to Dial Books for Young
Readers, a division of Penguin Books USA Inc., 375 Hudson Street,
New York, NY 10014.

ISBN 0-590-45772-1

Copyright © 1991 by Susan Jeffers.
All rights reserved. Published by Scholastic Inc.,
555 Broadway, New York, NY 10012, by arrangement with
Dial Books for Young Readers, a division of Penguin Books USA Inc.

12 11 10 9 8 7 6 5 4   7 8 9/9 0 1/0

Printed in the U.S.A.   08

First Scholastic printing, September 1996

The full-color artwork was prepared using a fine-line pen with ink and dyes.
They were applied over a detailed pencil drawing that was then erased.
The jacket art was based on a photograph
by Edward Curtis.

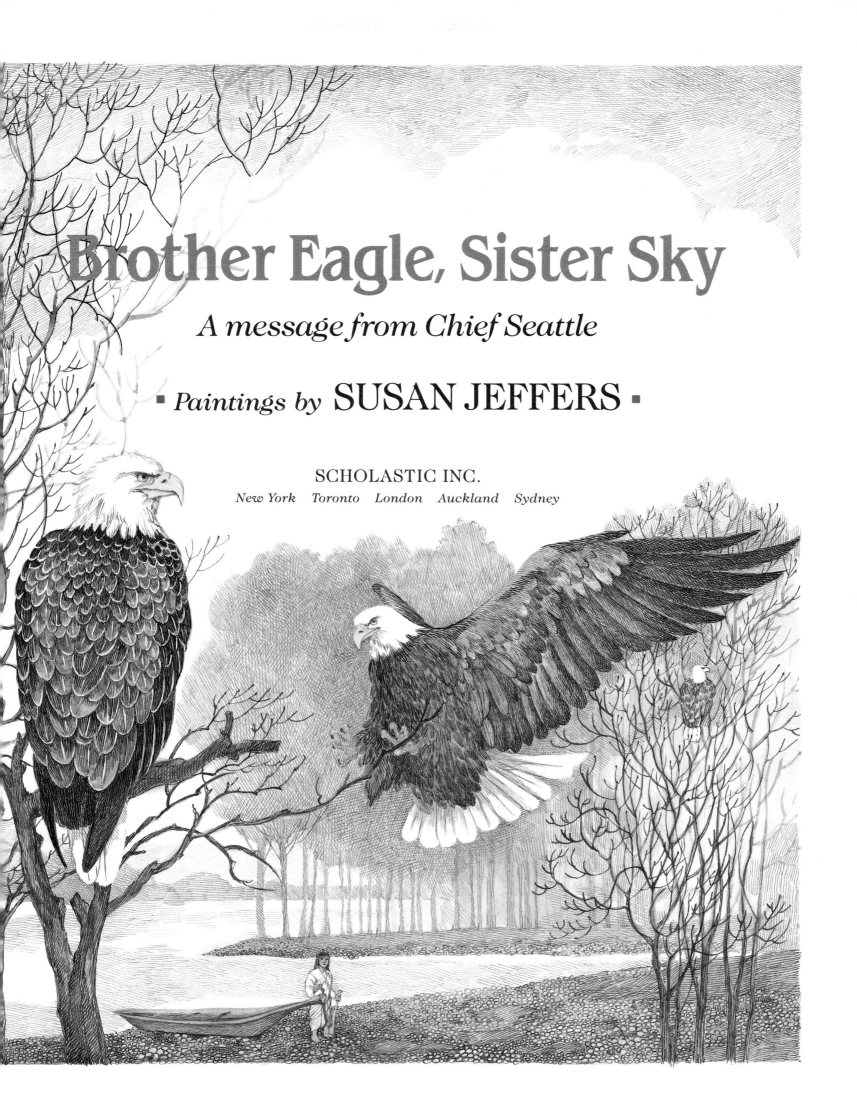

Brother Eagle, Sister Sky

A message from Chief Seattle

· Paintings *by* SUSAN JEFFERS ·

SCHOLASTIC INC.

New York   Toronto   London   Auckland   Sydney

In a time so long ago that nearly all traces of it are lost in the prairie dust, an ancient people were a part of the land that we love and call America. Living here for thousands of years, their children became the great Indian civilizations of the Choctaw and Cherokee, Navaho, Iroquois and Sioux, among many others. Then white settlers from Europe began a bloody war against the Indians, and in the span of a single lifetime claimed all the Indians' land for themselves, allowing them only small tracts of land to live on.

When the last of the Indian wars were drawing to a close, one of the bravest and most respected chiefs of the Northwest Nations, Chief Seattle, sat at a white man's table to sign a paper presented by the new Commissioner of Indian Affairs for the Territory. The government in Washington, D.C., wished to buy the lands of Chief Seattle's people.

With a commanding presence and eyes that mirrored the great soul that lived within, the Chief rose to speak to the gathering in a resounding voice.

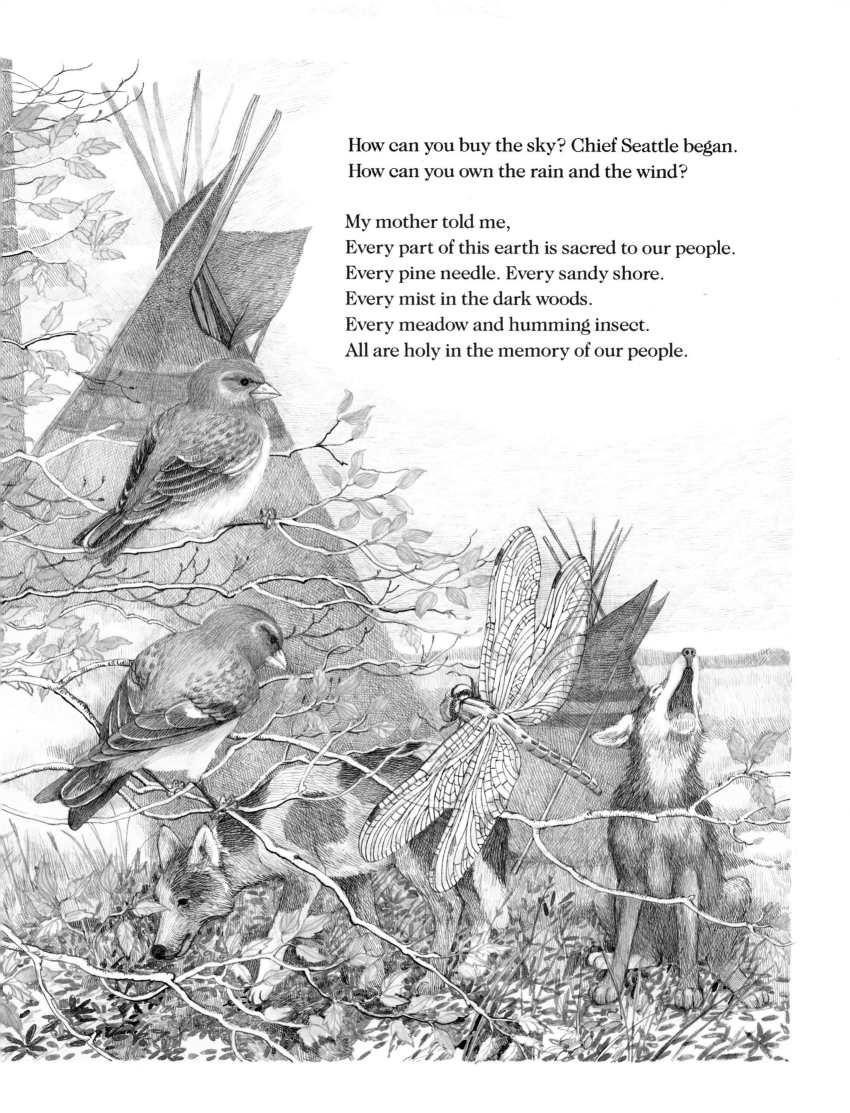

How can you buy the sky? Chief Seattle began.
How can you own the rain and the wind?

My mother told me,
Every part of this earth is sacred to our people.
Every pine needle. Every sandy shore.
Every mist in the dark woods.
Every meadow and humming insect.
All are holy in the memory of our people.

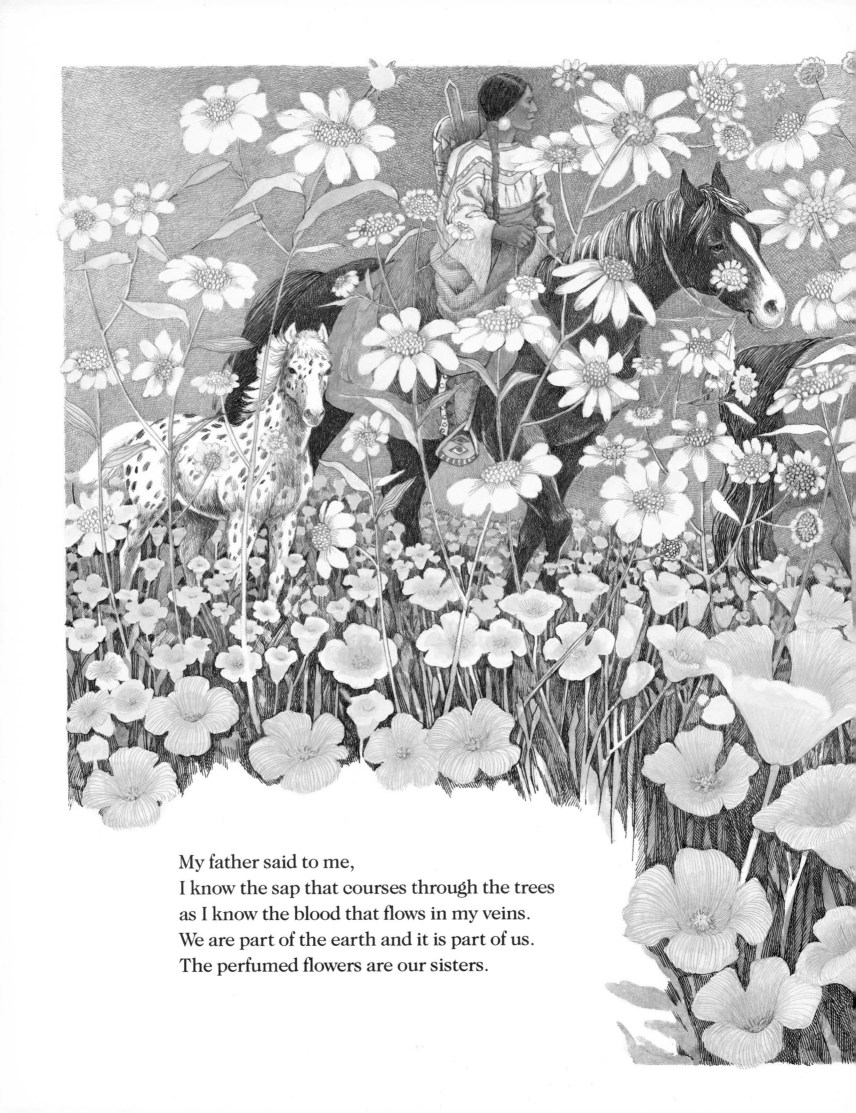

My father said to me,
I know the sap that courses through the trees
as I know the blood that flows in my veins.
We are part of the earth and it is part of us.
The perfumed flowers are our sisters.

The bear, the deer, the great eagle, these are our brothers.

The rocky crests, the meadows,
the ponies—all belong to the same family.

The voice of my ancestors said to me,
The shining water that moves in the streams and rivers is
not simply water, but the blood of your grandfather's grandfather.
Each ghostly reflection in the clear waters of the lakes tells
of memories in the life of our people.
The water's murmur is the voice of your great-great-grandmother.
The rivers are our brothers. They quench our thirst.
They carry our canoes and feed our children.
You must give to the rivers the kindness you would give
to any brother.

The voice of my grandfather said to me,
The air is precious. It shares its spirit with all
the life it supports. The wind that gave me my first
breath also received my last sigh.
You must keep the land and air apart and sacred,
as a place where one can go to taste the wind that
is sweetened by the meadow flowers.

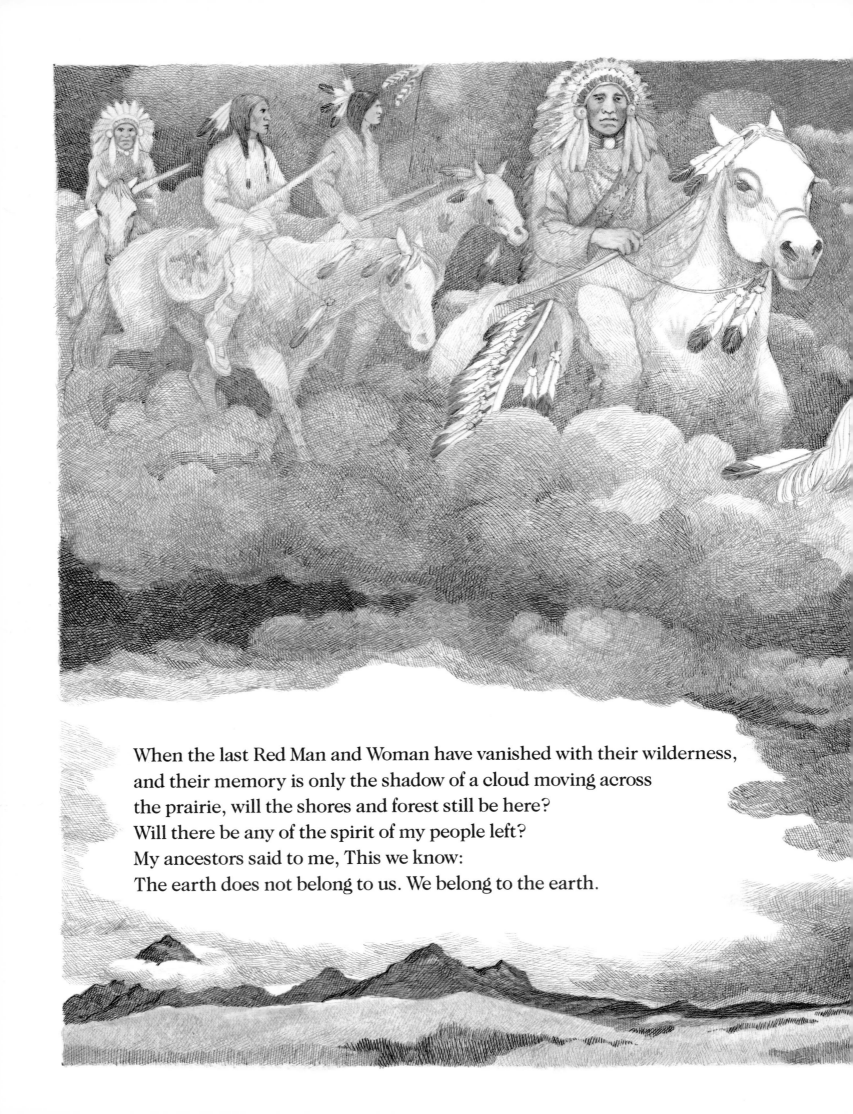

When the last Red Man and Woman have vanished with their wilderness,
and their memory is only the shadow of a cloud moving across
the prairie, will the shores and forest still be here?
Will there be any of the spirit of my people left?
My ancestors said to me, This we know:
The earth does not belong to us. We belong to the earth.